The White Horse Inn, Jackson Bridge, the 'Last of the Summer Wine Pub'.

Alan J W Bell, Producer/Director, who took over the series in 1981, was the first Producer/Director to introduce the full length film of the series. Alan has remained with the series through its most successful years.

Foreword

Holmfirth Photographer Malcolm Howarth.

Special occasions are always best remembered by photographs, so, when I took-over the production of 'Last of the Summer Wine' in 1981, I always carried a small 35mm camera with me to record happy moments during the six weeks of filming. For me, every day working on such a prestigious production in such a beautiful location was a really special occasion. The only trouble was that the best pictures were never taken because, obviously, the business of directing the filming was more pressing for me than taking background photographs. The BBC's own photographs understandably tended to be rather formal and feature the principal actors against the well-known Holmfirth locations. Nothing to remind one of an eventful day or a great achievement.

My choice of The White Horse Inn as a location at Jackson Bridge (just outside of Holmfirth) proved to be fortuitous, for the landlord's son, Paul Backhouse, was a keen photographer who soon provided scores of excellent pictures recording the progress of the filming. Through him, Malcolm Howarth entered the scene and soon became our Official Photographer. If there was an interesting stunt sequence, or simply a unit photograph with everyone from the stars to the drivers in it, Malcolm could always be relied upon to be there and perfectly capture the moment and the memory. Besides becoming invaluable as our photographer, Malcolm also helped us immensely in finding locations, and by being the programme's ambassador in the Holme Valley.

I hope that the photographs in this book give as much pleasure to others as they do to me, for they record the background to the making of television's longest running and best loved comedy series.

Alan J W Bell

A typical view across the valley at Holmfirth, so suitably chosen as the location for the series.

Victoria Square, Holmfirth - a West Yorkshire town set in a steep-sided valley with its own brand of architecture suited to the steep hills.

General Introduction to 'Last of the Summer Wine'

Author Roy Clarke on location.

Roy Clarke's professional writing career began in radio with two thriller serials (both produced by Alan Ayckbourn). His first work for television was an episode of 'The Troubleshooters' for BBC/TV, which introduced a character later developed by him into the celebrated Basil Allenby-Johnson as played by Ronald Fraser in two series of 'The Misfit' for ATV, winning the Writers' Guild Award as Best Series of 1970. He also won the Royal Television Society's Award in 1975, and both the Pye and Radio Industry Awards in 1982.

He has written several single plays, a few drama series and situation comedies, including 'Open All Hours' starring Ronnie Barker, proving he has achieved the rare distinction of writing equally successfully for both television drama and situation comedy.

Both 'Last of the Summer Wine' and 'Open All Hours' have consistently topped the ratings charts since 1982. 'Last of the Summer Wine' won the Radio Industries Award for 1982 and was also voted favourite comedy series in the 1982 Multicoloured Swapshop Awards. Roy Clarke also scored a double in winning the Pye Colour Television Award for Best Written Comedy for 'Last of the Summer Wine' and came joint third in the same category for 'Open All Hours'. Both series were also shortlisted in the 1985 BAFTA Awards for Best Comedy Programme.

Roy Clarke has completed work on an original film drama series 'Pulaski', also for BBC/TV. His most recent work includes two series of 'First of the Summer Wine', which deals with Summer Wine characters in their youthful days around 1939, and more recently the BBC comedy series 'Keeping Up Appearances'.

Summer Wine Characters

Peter Sallis alias 'Norman Clegg'. (Above) Peter admits that Norman Clegg is his favourite character in his varied career on stage and screen. Peter loves working in Holmfirth even if it is just to visit his favourite book shops. His many films include 'Saturday Night and Sunday Morning', 'Wuthering Heights' and 'Witness for the Prosecution'. His television appearances over the years, which include 'Dr Who' and 'Callan', are certainly too many to list.

Brian Wilde alias 'Foggy Dewhurst'. (Right) Brian, who plays the part of military minded Foggy Dewhurst, says that Foggy is quite a harmless chap, basically just very silly. A veteran 'Summer Wine' character, Brian recently re-appeared for his second stint. He admits to liking Holmfirth and its scenery, but is none too keen on the unpredictable Yorkshire weather. The BBC series 'Porridge' also gave Brian fame as the Prison Warder who had to contend with Fletcher, played by Ronnie Barker.

THIS SECTION OF THE BOOK DEALS WITH THE CHARACTERS WHO ARE PRESENTLY CONTRIBUTING TO THE PROGRAMME'S SUCCESS.

Compo Simonite played by actor Bill Owen. (Above) Bill Owen MBE, a native of London's East End, is now an official Yorkshireman; in 1990 the Yorkshire Society made him an honorary Yorkshireman. His past acting career includes so many successes that there would be simply not enough room to list them in this book. He has also written over 90 songs which have all been recorded and include 'Broken Hearted' by Ken Dodd, 'Baby I Love You' by Sacha Distel, 'So Lucky' by Al Martino and 'So Little Time' by Matt Munro. If that is not enough Bill is also a successful playwright.

Nora Batty played by actress Kathy Staff. (Above) Nora Batty complete with wrinkled stockings, the most unlikely pin-up complete with apron and curlers, frightens the life out of the male population. Kathy, a very popular actress, has delighted thousands of fans with her regular appearances on the programme. A career which started in 1949 with Weekly Repertory Company has since included many varied roles; appearing in 'Coronation Street', in 'Open All Hours' as Mrs Blewitt and as Doris Luke in 'Crossroads'. Again as with other 'Summer Wine' actors her list of successes in the acting profession would be quite long and impressive.

Thora Hird as Edie. *(Below, left in photo) The dearly loved and well known actress Thora Hird stated publicly that 'Summer Wine' was her favourite programme. An invitation to play the part of Edie in a special film resulted in a regular slot and she has stayed with the series ever since. Morecambe born, Thora has brought pleasure to millions in a stage and television career spanning over 60 years. Apart from 'Summer Wine' her recent successes include 'In Loving Memory', part of which was filmed in Holmfirth's neighbouring town Slaithwaite. Thora can still be seen every Sunday enjoying the hymns in 'Songs of Praise'.*

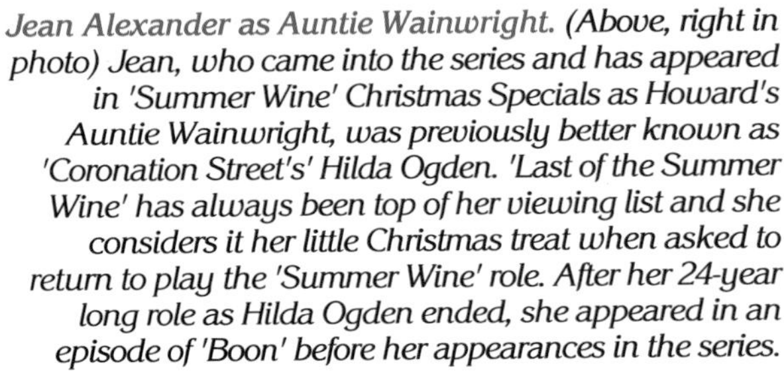

Jean Alexander as Auntie Wainwright. *(Above, right in photo) Jean, who came into the series and has appeared in 'Summer Wine' Christmas Specials as Howard's Auntie Wainwright, was previously better known as 'Coronation Street's' Hilda Ogden. 'Last of the Summer Wine' has always been top of her viewing list and she considers it her little Christmas treat when asked to return to play the 'Summer Wine' role. After her 24-year long role as Hilda Ogden ended, she appeared in an episode of 'Boon' before her appearances in the series.*

Jane Freeman as Ivy. *(Left) Long suffering cafe owner Ivy, played by actress Jane Freeman, has become a popular household name. Jane has extensive repertory experience spanning the length and breadth of the country. Her recent work has included a national tour of 'When We Are Married' whilst her many television credits include 'Crossroads', 'Within These Walls' and several other BBC productions. Jane always enjoys a very busy regular pantomime season. Unlike her role as Ivy, Jane is a lovely gentle lady, as are all of the female cast of 'Last of the Summer Wine'.*

Gordon Wharmby as Wesley. (Right) Wesley is in love, but not with his domineering wife Edie in the programme; his passion is for fiddling with an old car engine. Gordon came to acting late in life but immediately realised that was the life for him - he thoroughly enjoys his 'Summer Wine' filming sessions.

Marina, the ageing 'femme fatale', played by Jean Ferguson. (Below) Jean, who has been quite a busy actress, admits, to having spent many happy hours working on 'Last of the Summer Wine' in the Holmfirth area. Says Jean: "I'm so very grateful to the programme for introducing me to some of the most warm and generous people that it has been my pleasure to meet anywhere in the world".

Robert Fyfe plays Howard. (Above) Robert Fyfe, another busy actor, is no stranger to West Yorkshire. In his years as a drama student in Bradford he spent his weekends walking the moors in North Yorkshire, but had never experienced the beauty of Holmfirth's moorland. "The sun doesn't always shine on film-makers but the welcome we are given by the people of Holmfirth and friends of the programme more than makes up for the occasional drenching - even for falling in the canal".

Sarah Thomas as Glenda. (Left) Sarah, appearing in J B Priestley's 'When We Are Married', received a phone-call from Alan Bell offering her a part alongside Thora Hird in the 'Last of the Summer Wine' series. Since then Sarah has been a regular in the programme and admits she has spent many happy hours working alongside the famous 'Summer Wine' cast and experiencing the magic of the Holmfirth hills.

Juliette Kaplan as Pearl. *(Left) Juliette Kaplan was thrilled to be offered the part of Pearl in 'Last of the Summer Wine'. Her thoughts of the North were always grey, drab and smokey, but like many others of the cast she was very surprised at the rolling hills and different shades of green and gold in the fields. When she first arrived on the train her first experience of the Yorkshire friendliness was the accent to greet her, belonging to a burly smiling-eyed man who said "Them bags are too heavy for thee lass, I'll tak'em".*

Michael Grady as Barry. *(Above) Michael Grady was first introduced to the series as Barry, who was soon to marry Glenda, the daughter of Edie in the programme. Barry was soon involved in the zany stunts of the trio by Uncle Seymour. Michael's other television appearances have included a role in the popular television series 'Citizen Smith'.*

Danny O'Dea as Eli. *(Right) Danny is a much loved and experienced actor whose days on the stage could fill a book twice over. Danny, a gentleman in real life, plays the part of short-sighted Eli and regularly amuses our famous trio with his antics. The only time a pub empties before time is called is when Eli picks up a set of darts.*

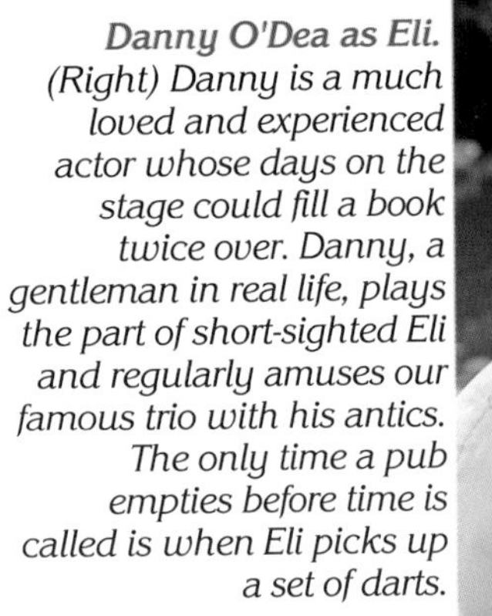

Cardew Robinson (Cardew the Cad) as Gough. *(Below) A guest appearance when he played a henpecked husband in 'Gough and Jessies's Golden Wedding'. 'Summer Wine' has slotted in many other famous faces over the years.*

Stephen Lewis as Smiler. *(Left) Stephen's most memorable role was that of Inspector Blake in the favourite comedy series 'On The Buses'. He was introduced to 'Summer Wine' in 1991 as Smiler - Nora Batty's lodger. Not popular at all with Compo!*

Vintage Summer Wine

THIS SECTION GIVES A BRIEF HISTORY OF THE PROGRAMME.

(Above) Clegg, Compo and Blamire at Sid's Cafe.

'Last of the Summer Wine' first began in June 1971, when a film crew arrived in Holmfirth to shoot location scenes for a 'pilot' (single episode) to be included in a very popular series at the time, entitled 'Comedy Playhouse'. The author was Roy Clarke. The Producer/Director was James Gilbert.

The three leading players were:
Michael Bates as Blamire,
Peter Sallis as Clegg,
Bill Owen as Compo,
with Kathy Staff as Nora Batty, Jane Freeman as Ivy and John Comer as Sid, her husband.
The 'pilot' was shown in 'Comedy Playhouse' on January 4th 1972. A series was commissioned and shown in 1973.

(Left) Michael Bates as 'Blamire'. Michael Bates was a brilliant actor, who will most certainly be remembered as Punkah-Wallah in 'It Ain't Half Hot Mum'.

(Left) Clegg, Compo and Blamire pictured on one of their frequent visits to the library. A room at Holmfirth Methodist Church was converted to look like the town's library.

Sadly, Michael Bates died in 1975. In view of his impressive performance as Blamire, serious consideration was given to ending the series. However, in view of its growing popularity it was decided to continue and a new character was introduced in the person of Foggy Dewhurst played by Brian Wilde. Sydney Lotterby, Producer/Director of many successful comedy series, including 'Yes Minister', took over 'Last of the Summer Wine'.

(Main Picture) Clegg, Compo and Blamire no doubt discussing plotting another adventure.

(Left) Ivy and Sid, Jane Freeman and John Comer, pictured at Sid's Cafe which became the favourite hang-out for the loony trio. John Comer, alias Sid, played the part of the typical husband whose wife always keeps a tight rein on him; very rarely was he allowed to mix with the famous three.

(Above) Compo pictured with man-eater Lily Blesser in the first full-length film simply entitled 'Last of the Summer Wine', from the original book by Roy Clarke. Lily Blesser was played by Linda Barron, who will always be remembered as Nurse Gladys Emmanuel in 'Open All Hours' with Ronnie Barker and David Jason.

A scene from the first full-length 'Last of the Summer Wine' film. A film crew shoot a scene involving Sid's mobile chippy.

Foggy, Compo and Clegg (Above) Brian Wilde joined the series in 1976 playing the character of Foggy Dewhurst. Foggy was a regular Corporal Sign Writer who returns to his home town after being retired from the army.

(Below) Hen-pecked Wally Batty, alias Joe Gladwin. Joe will always be remembered for the nostalgic cameos in the famous series of brown bread commercials. Joe, born in Salford like many people on the other side of the Pennines, simply did not realise what beautiful countryside the Holme Valley had to offer. The filming of 'Summer Wine' had been amongst the happiest period of his long comedy career. Joe managed to engage our sympathies as Wally Batty until 1986, when at the age of 82, he sadly passed away.

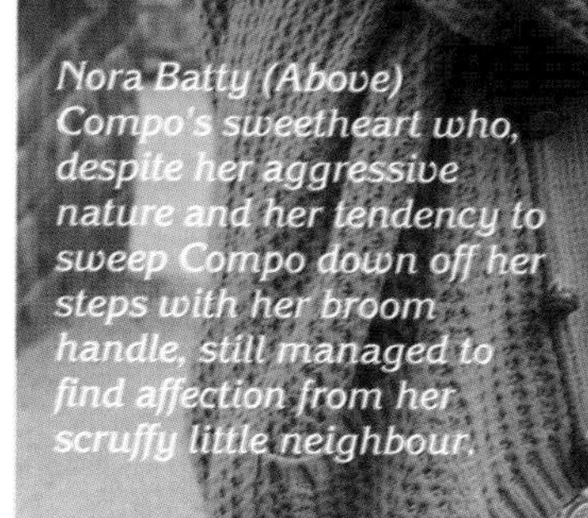
Nora Batty (Above) Compo's sweetheart who, despite her aggressive nature and her tendency to sweep Compo down off her steps with her broom handle, still managed to find affection from her scruffy little neighbour.

(Above) Compo and Nora with the matchbox. Compo's matchbox, the contents of which have never been revealed to the viewers, began to find a regular appearance in the programme. Compo, in the moments of boredom or in the middle of someone else's serious conversations, whipped out his matchbox to startle everyone with its contents.

The cafe situated in the church square is actually set out just as it is in the programme, where visitors can enjoy a hot meal and a cuppa. Not always a cafe, it has been a fish and chip shop and when filming first began was a store room for the local Ironmongers. Only in the last few years has it become a cafe and successfully caters for thousands of 'Summer Wine' fans visiting the town each year.

Most of the programmes' plots were hatched out during a cup of tea and a bun at Sid's Cafe.

(Below) Sid and Ivy pictured on location at The White Horse Inn, Jackson Bridge. Shortly after filming this series John Comer sadly passed away. From then on Ivy ran the cafe on her own and from that point it was known as Ivy's Cafe.

13

It was a rare occasion, indeed if ever, that Compo would receive such a loving hug from Nora. Many is the time that the viewing public has been willing Nora to give in to Compo's advances, but so far she has managed to resist his charms, if he has any!

Foggy Leaves

Brian Wilde left the series in 1984, and was replaced by the well-known actor Michael Aldridge, who came direct from his other TV series 'Charters and Caldecotes' and so the public met Seymour. Alan Bell who took over the series in 1981, was the first Producer/Director to introduce the full length TV film of the series, the second of which, 'Uncle of the Bride', introduced Seymour to the viewers. Also introduced in 'Uncle of the Bride' was the well known actress Thora Hird, who had stated publicly that this was her favourite TV programme and she would love to play in it, and the two newly weds: Sarah Thomas and Michael Grady 'Glenda and Barry'.

(Above) A scene from 'Uncle of the Bride' which introduced the character of Professor Seymour Utterthwaite played by Michael Aldridge. Michael, a Shakespearian actor, is again one of the many of the cast of 'Summer Wine' who have made several other TV appearances.

(Right) Trio with tools; Clegg and Compo never seem to have any confidence in any of Seymour's inventions and Compo more often than not ended up regretting ever getting involved. Seymour treated Compo as his 'guinea pig' or 'test pilot'.

(Below) Wesley (Gordon Wharmby) usually found himself as engineer working from the professor's drawings for his unusual inventions. Wesley could hardly refuse Seymour's request as he was his brother-in-law. Wesley's wife Edie made sure that anything 'our' Seymour wanted 'our' Seymour got.

(Below) Clegg and Compo pictured at Seymour's house just after meeting Seymour for the first time.

Foggy Returns

Michael Aldridge left the programme in 1990. No sooner had Clegg and Compo packed Seymour on the bus than the familiar face of Foggy appeared on the next. Brian Wilde had returned to the programme in the first episode of a new series entitled 'Return of the Warrior'. Foggy had returned after a period of decorating eggs in Scarborough and was soon back in charge of the boys, frequently demonstrating his military abilities.

(Above) Foggy arrives back to his home town and immediately commands attention.

(Right above and Right below) Compo and Clegg relax after evading Foggy on one of his route marches, leaving Foggy still briskly walking on talking to himself.

(Below) A scene from 'Come-in Sun Ray Major' where another of Foggy's bright ideas fails.

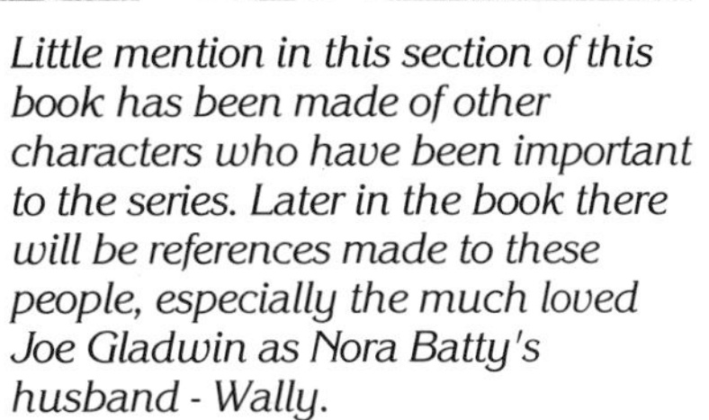

Little mention in this section of this book has been made of other characters who have been important to the series. Later in the book there will be references made to these people, especially the much loved Joe Gladwin as Nora Batty's husband - Wally.

THIS SECTION INCLUDES HOLMFIRTH SCENERY WITH CAST AND CREW.

No Wonder Holmfirth

(Above) A view towards Holme Moss from Holme village which looks down over Holmfirth. There are several different walks in these areas, each of which has a unique peaceful beauty.

(Above and right) Digley Reservoir situated above Holmfirth. The above photo is a mirror image across the reservoir taken during January. Even the winter months still give a magical beauty.

(Left) Holmfirth Parish Church with Clegg's house situated to the right-hand side of the church belfry. Recently the location for Clegg's and Howard and Pearl's houses has moved to Jackson Bridge to a pretty row of weavers' cottages on the hillside above the White Horse Inn.

(Left) Nora Batty's house with Nora's red bucket waiting on the steps. Next door to Nora's can be found the Wrinkled Stocking Tearoom, in which visitors to Holmfirth can enjoy their favourite cuppa and can remember scenes from their favourite episodes filmed on Nora Batty's steps.

(Below) Bill Owen relaxes between scenes high in the hills at one of many picturesque streams.

(Left) The Packhorse Bridge at Marsden, one of many beauty spots around the 'Summer Wine' town.

(Below) Another Holmfirth hilltop above New Mill. This beautiful hilltop, known to locals as Tinker's Monument, is extensively used for many of the stunt sequences.

High in the hills above Holmfirth. A view from Holme Village looking down on Holmbridge, Upperthong and Holmfirth further down the valley.

(Above) Compo, Clegg and Seymour pictured at Windscar Reservoir.

(Right) 'Old Genn' in Towngate, Holmfirth - commemorating the Peace of Amiens in the Napoleonic Wars, and also the height of the 1852 Flood.

The hills around Holmfirth have several reservoirs, each of which has its own beauty and is quite an attraction for locals and visitors alike. However, one such dam, the Bilberry Reservoir, caused the biggest damburst disaster in British history. The attention of the whole country was focused on Holmfirth in 1852 when, after several days of heavy rain, the banks burst on the night of February 5th. This created havoc throughout the whole of the Holme Valley, where 81 people lost their lives. Mills, houses, bridges all disappeared and the valley was never to be the same again. 4,898 adults and 2,142 children were put out of work as a direct result of the disaster.

(Above) A hang-gliding experience for Barry in the country roads at Jackson Bridge.

Not the only Floods

The Holmfirth Great Flood of 1777, caused by an almighty thunderstorm on the hills above the town, led to the loss of three lives and extensive damage. A lettered stone showing the height of the water may be seen at the back of the boot and shoe shop in Cheapside, Towngate.

On June 10th 1944, the Holmfirth Express reported that sightseers from many parts of the country travelled to Holmfirth to witness the widespread destruction caused by the Whit Monday cloudburst. The River Holme rose to a height of more than 18 feet and the raging torrents sweeping down the valley destroyed mills and bridges with the loss of three lives.

(Left and Below) The filming of 'Summer Wine' is largely within a radius of 7 or 8 miles of Holmfirth. One of the popular locations is the Packhorse Bridge at Marsden.

A Pleasure for Filming

(Left) A still summer's day, warm sunshine and time to relax between shots. Perfect conditions for the film-maker. But the hills of Holmfirth don't always offer such comforts as the weather can alter dramatically within minutes.

(Below) The production team left to right, Production Manager, John Gorringe; Production Assistant, Petra Collier; Production Manager, Duncan Cooper; Producer/Director, Alan J W Bell; Assistant Floor Managers, Mark Mylod and Rachel Dison.

(Above) A quiet beauty spot in the valley below the Woodhead Pass. The 'Summer Wine' production team finds time for a joke on their way back to the catering unit at lunch-time. The team appear to be hanging on by their fingernails after a steep climb out of the valley. Whilst this picture was being taken Peter Sallis appeared from his caravan and, looking amazed at the team hanging on over the edge, held up his empty dinner plate and said with typical Clegg humour "hands up all those who haven't had lunch".

(Left and Above) The crew on location at Tinker's Monument in the hills above the 'Summer Wine' pub at Jackson Bridge. A shower arrives right in the middle of a lengthy scene and the crew and actors have to wait in their positions until the rain dies off.

Even on a summer's day the temperature on the hills can drop dramatically and the crew in the discomfort of the biting cold wind still have the hard task of convincing the viewers that it is a bright warm summer day. Pictured filming the barrel rolling sequence in 'Roll On' filmed in 1990 are: Film Cameraman, Mike Radford and Producer/Director, Alan J W Bell.

Flaming June

(Left) June 5th 1990 on Cartworth Moor, two miles above the town during filming of 'Charity Balls'. Kathy Staff and Jane Freeman sit huddled together in bitterly cold winter conditions, frozen to the bone despite the padding, costumes, coats and blankets.

Mike Radford

(Right, Far right and Below) Filming has to continue even in the short gaps between showers. Cycling sequence with Compo, Clegg and Seymour.

Filming at Nora Batty's House

(Above) Film cameraman, Alan Stevens.

(Right) Wally and Nora - Nora has searched everywhere for Wally all day, but still won't admit she has missed him.

(Above) Nora getting Wally from under her feet.

(Left) Nora Batty on the look-out for strange neighbours.

(Below) Assistant Cameraman, John Sennet and Assistant Cameraman, Robert S McDonald.

(Below) Nora shows off her wrinkled stockings whilst Wally's only interest is to comfort his whippet.

(Bottom left) Smiler is locked out - Compo to the rescue.

Filming at the Cafe

Many a mile of film was used in scenes at the cafe. Remember Crusher Milburn played by Jonathan Linsley, who came to the cafe to 'learn the business' and to help his Auntie Ivy?

(Above) Nora, Crusher and Ivy - Crusher was frightened of no man but his Auntie and Nora Batty were something different.

(Left) Jane Freeman (Ivy) with her freshly baked butterfly buns which even Nora cannot resist.

(Right) Ivy gives her nephew strict instructions although she was never sure whether the information was sinking in or not.

(Below) Once again the cafe is the central scene for another plot which involved passing on a secret message from Marina to Howard.

Compo once again tries to impress Nora Batty in 'The Last Surviving Maurice Chevalier Impression'.

Not all 'Summer Wine' has been about the summer-time; there have been many Christmas episodes, one of which was (Left) 'Merry Christmas Father Christmas'. Cameraman Alan Stevens and Alan J W Bell rehearse with the actors for this special Christmas episode. Note the leaves on the trees. This episode was shot during the summer months and the village of Jackson Bridge, location for this scene, was covered in snow to give the winter appearance by Special Effects Designer, Chris Lawton.

(Right) Christmas episode of 1989 - cast and crew pictured at Auntie Wainwright's shop.

(Bottom left) Pearl, Edie and Glenda with Auntie Wainwright.

(Bottom right) Christmas special 'What's Santa Brought For Nora Then?'. The children of Marsden Junior School providing the carols.

(Left) Edie Pegden with daughter Glenda. Edie is explaining to her daughter Glenda how to keep her father Wesley's greasy boots out of the house.

(Right) Cast and crew set up a typical scene outside the Pegdens'.

Filming at the Pegdens'

(Below) Wesley studies a problem with his Land Rover's engine.

(Below) Seymour discusses with Wesley the details of another hare-brained invention.

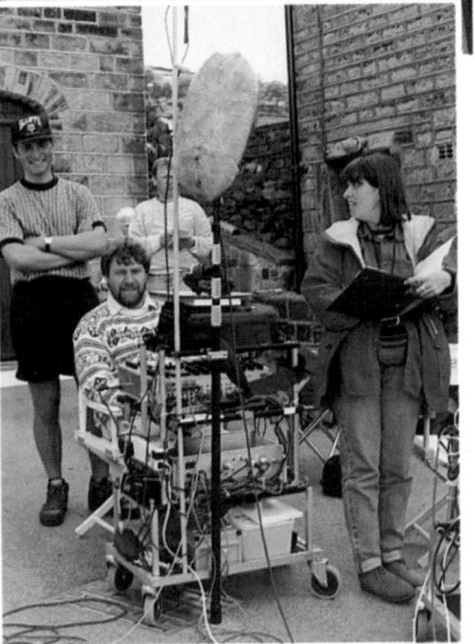

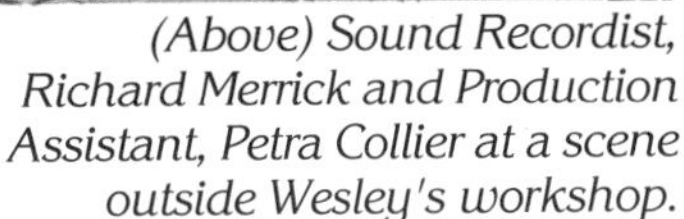

(Above) Sound Recordist, Richard Merrick and Production Assistant, Petra Collier at a scene outside Wesley's workshop.

(Below) Wesley, with strict instructions to keep himself clean, finds himself once again in the thick of trouble.

(Above) Clegg and Compo look on with disbelief as Wesley completes work on Seymour's sub-aqua scrutiniser (suitable for locating misplaced dentures, supermarket trolleys and old mattresses etc. in the local canal).

1987: the third TV special, 'Big Day At Dream Acres'. A selection of pictures from this episode; as usual the day starts with a knock on someone's door, a lot of walking, talking and drinking, the odd bad-tempered moment and always the guarantee of mishap, mayhem and misfortune.

Big Day at Dream Acres

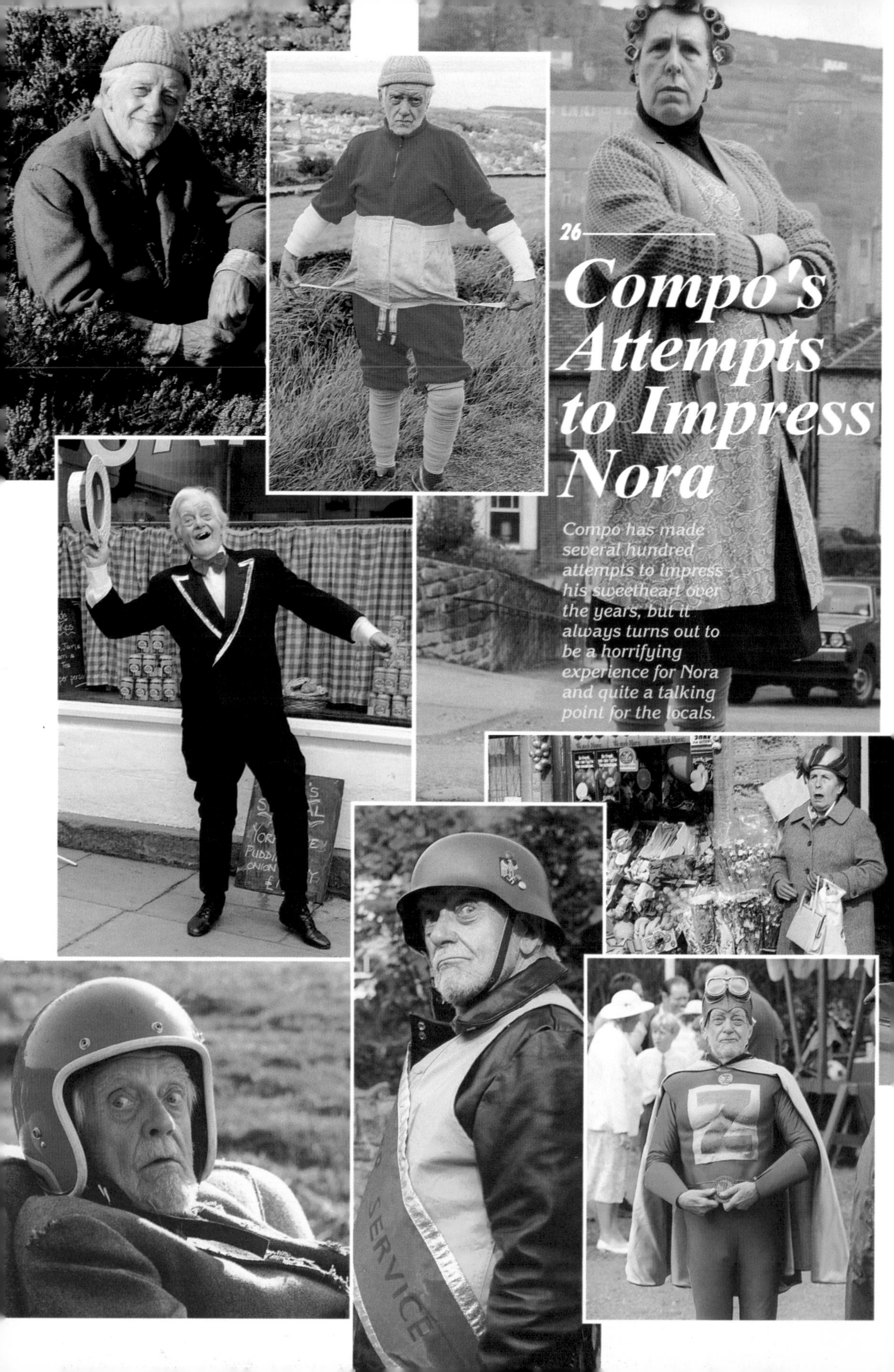

26

Compo's Attempts to Impress Nora

Compo has made several hundred attempts to impress his sweetheart over the years, but it always turns out to be a horrifying experience for Nora and quite a talking point for the locals.

Crew and cast 1990

Crew and cast 1991

'Roll On'

(Left) Wesley unknowingly gets himself involved.

(Below) Edie cannot believe her eyes.

After sessions filming in the beautiful Yorkshire hills and valleys there are always studio sessions with a live audience to complete the show.

(Above) Studio set at Edie's house picturing Edie and Glenda preparing for the daily ladies' chinwag.

(Right) Studio set of Gough and Jessie's Golden Wedding with waitress Nora Batty putting the boys in order. (Bottom photos) Further scenes from this set.

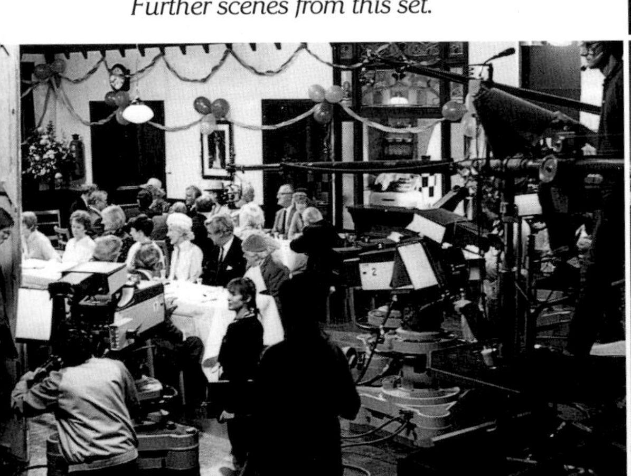

Pearl threatens Howard with her pruning shears.

The surprised look when discovered in a remote country spot.

Howard (Robert Fyfe), his wife Pearl (Juliette Kaplan) and Howard's lady companion Marina (Jean Ferguson) have added much to the excitement of the series.

A timid, hen-pecked man always under the careful watch of Pearl, his wife, who tends to hear every word he says and finds him more jobs than enough to fill his day. Surprisingly, he still finds time to disappear into the countryside with his beloved Marina. Many disguises have been used to avoid recognition but somehow fate always seems to put them into the path of our three heroes.

Sometimes the disguise interferes with their love life.

(Above) Speeding off before Pearl spots them.

(Right) Even dressed as Secret Agents they failed to fool anyone.

Scenes from some of the latest episodes

(Right) Eli accidentally chains himself to the railings instead of his bike.

(Above) Eli with his dog.

Edie, Ivy and Nora's lodger Smiler take a break from church cleaning duties to investigate the screams of Nora Batty.

(Above) Compo tries to grab Nora from behind a gravestone.

(Left) The helmet is too small but Foggy's military experience comes in handy.

(Right) Foggy convinces Compo that he could become an expert pole vaulter.